The *Make-up* Artist

The Make-up Artist

FINDING GOD'S NATURAL BEAUTY IN YOU

Dorothy Brown

PALMETTO
PUBLISHING
Charleston, SC
www.PalmettoPublishing.com

Copyright © 2024 by Dorothy Brown

All rights reserved

No portion of this book may be reproduced, stored in a retrieval system, or transmitted in any form by any means–electronic, mechanical, photocopy, recording, or other–except for brief quotations in printed reviews, without prior permission of the author.

Paperback ISBN: 979-8-8229-5107-5

TABLE OF CONTENTS

Introduction	vii
Finding God's Natural Beauty in You	ix
Part One	1
Chapter One: From Glory to Glory	3
Chapter Two: Finding the Oil	6
Chapter Three: Beauty vs. Glory	10
Chapter Four: What's Eating You?	12
Chapter Five: Chosen for Greatness	14
Chapter Six: Fixed in the Valley	19
Chapter Seven: A New Creature	24
Part Two	27
Chapter One: The Beast Within	29
Chapter Two: Stay Focused	31
Chapter Three: Unwanted Fruit	34
Chapter Four: Kill the Beast	38
Chapter Five: Let Go and Let God	44
Chapter Six: Resist, Refuse, and Revoke	49
Part Three	53
Chapter One: The Queen in You	55
Chapter Two: Seasons	60

Chapter Three: Timing	63
Chapter Four: The Set Place	66
Chapter Five: Where Does Your Strength Lie?	69
Chapter Six: Sold Out!	72
Part Four	75
Chapter One: Highly Favored	77
Chapter Two: Trust God and Go!	81
Chapter Three: Boot Camp	85
Chapter Four: It's Not About You	88
Chapter Five: A Precious Jewel (Favor)	91
Chapter Six: Is That Your Oil?	94
Chapter Seven: Finish Your Assignment	96
Acknowledgments	101

Introduction

For whatever reason, at some point in life, we lose sight as to what is important and what is detrimental to us. Life is full of crooks and turns, with many distractions. Therefore, if we want to follow the path that is set before us by God, it is imperative that we stay focused and ready to follow the instructions of God. What we want and what we cling to in life can either be beneficial or detrimental to us. This is why we must be very careful what we hope for on this journey. We should always want the perfect will of God so that our prayers are "yes" and "amen" and that our seeds are blessed down to the fourth generation! We should always know who we are and whose we are so that we aren't misguided by the adversary. Life is precious, and we should do the very best we can to make full use of it.

FINDING GOD'S
NATURAL BEAUTY IN YOU

Who is doing your makeup?

Out of all the name brands of makeup we have access to today, ladies, none of them holds light to the true beauty most of us possess on the inside. The inner beauty I am speaking of is the beauty of holiness that can only be obtained by a relationship with Jesus Christ. "This beauty, no makeup can alter or put it to shame." There is nothing wrong or sinful about adding to the beauty we already possess. Nevertheless, we should be mindful as to where our true beauty originates from. Beauty does not start in a bottle or on the tip of eyeliner, nor does it start with a favorite color of lipstick. All of these beauty products are vain and can sometimes be somewhat deceiving.

There is nothing wrong with adding color to your water; just make sure the water is purified before display. How many times have we as women stood in front of the mirror time after time to put on our makeup to beautify ourselves? For whatever reason we chose to do so, we must keep in mind what is true beauty. After we have smeared our faces with different shades of makeup, we examine our skin to make sure all makeup is evenly applied and our skin is covered to perfection. We lift our chin, turn our heads from left to right, and bow our necks just to make sure our makeover is perfect. We prance in the mirrors in the mornings for thirty minutes or more just to make sure our faces are picture-perfect. We want assurance that when we step out in public, we are looking fabulous! We look to encounter compliments, stares, and even a little envy from others.

Part One

CHAPTER ONE:

From Glory to Glory

After we have judged our beauty in our mirrors, I have to ask a question: Who is doing our makeup on the inside of us? Who or what is responsible for making up the inner us? What we must realize is that the only beauty that makes a difference in life is the beauty of holiness. If we don't have the true beauty of holiness, then all else we possess is null and void. The bible never mentioned anything about the outer beauty being the basis of our relationship with God.

The bible clearly states that God is concerned about the matters of the heart. No matter how long our hair is, how straight our teeth are, or how fair our skin is, it all goes back to what we possess on the inside. No matter how much external makeup we wear, it is not the mechanism that causes us to walk in the righteousness of God and precedes our place in heaven. If our outer appearance mattered to God, then he would have portioned us all the same amount of beauty.

When God's beauty rests upon us, it causes great and unusual things to happen in our lives. What happens as we attempt to draw near to God? He will draw near to us, causing a supernatural light to come upon us that cannot be explained by the carnal mind. Only those who have come in contact with or have a relationship with God will be able to tell where the light comes from. We may not see it, but others we meet and associate with do notice it. We can profess we are holy, act as if we are holy, but when there is true holiness in our lives, we don't have to say or act. Others will see it because it is a part of us. One thing I have noticed these days in Christendom is too many of us are acting like Pharaoh's boys; we are imitating righteousness and holiness. We talk a good game but don't possess the power that is willed to us by the Holy Ghost. Everything we do in God is by his power. When we love, it is by God's power. When we forgive, it is by his power. When we live a holy and righteous life , it is by his power. As the magicians did when trying to outcast Moses, God's messenger, this is what has happened in the church today. We have the dance, the preach, the wave, the cry, and yes, we also have the prophecies down pat. But sadly to say, some of these acts are just what they are: acts. In one instance, when Moses went up in the mountain to be with God, he came back with something the people had never seen and feared it. This that they saw was the glory of God resting heavy on Moses. The glory rested so until the children of Israel feared.

There was a supernatural glow on Moses because he had been in the presence of God (Exodus 34:29, 30). The first thing we need to understand is that Moses had a relationship with God, which caused an encounter with God. There is no way we can go to God time after time and nothing happens in our life. When we say we belong to God, there should be some evidence. When we stand before God on several occasions, something great on the inside should flourish in our lives. When we claim to have been in the presence of God and there is no evidence, then it becomes questionable as to where and what presence we have entertained. It is debatable as to who is doing our makeup. Ladies, if you really want to be attractive, I dare you to get in the presence of God. Allow God to beautify you in such a way that all will see the God in you. We make ourselves attractive so we might catch the eye of a good man and a God man, but what are we bringing to the table? Are we bringing the makeup, or are we coming made up with the things of God? We say many times we want a good man, but a wholesome, holy man is attracted to the God in our lives first. If there is no evidence of God in our lives, then that man will keep looking for his good thing. A good, God-fearing man will look past our flaws and see what he needs, and that is the God in us. He will see the comfort he will need, the ministry, the friendship, the consolation, and the correction he won't think he needs, also in a woman of God. A good, God-fearing man can see the heart through the makeup. The discernment of God he has obtained through a relationship with God will allow him to see it. We can smile, look holy, and act holy, but an eagle eye of discernment will call it out every time. If you feel you should be chosen by the bishop's son because you look good, but he never gives you a second look, don't get mad. First, you may not be the one God has chosen for him. Second, you may not have the right makeup artist. Before we begin to think so highly of ourselves, we need to be sure of what we possess on the inside. Some of the entities we possess are not so holy, and we know it. I know a few of us may think we are pretty enough to get what we want, but it does not work that way with God.

CHAPTER TWO:
Finding the Oil

When Samuel seemingly went to seek a king, he thought that great statue and good looks indicated kingship. Samuel thought he'd hit the nail on the head, but God refused the first one, Eliab. Then there were more that were brought before Samuel. Everyone in the house was refused, only because God was looking for someone who had the right makeup. He wanted someone who had him on his mind day and night. He was looking for someone who did not need an audience. Therefore, God had to speak to Samuel to say, "Beauty is not what I am looking for. In essence, there is a war out there, and good looks won't get it." God said, "Don't look at how tall he is or how handsome he is." God wanted someone who knew about relationships. God wanted someone who knew how to provoke him to bless him.

The oil was not to be poured until the right man for the position was present. No one was worthy of the oil—only the one who was after the heart of God (1 Samuel 16:11). Samuel asked to see if there was someone else he could take a look at (verse 12). David was brought in, probably well-worked and tired. Although David was out in the field in all the dust and dung, he was still attractive. David was beautiful from the inside out because of his relationship with God. Out of all that dust, grim, the word of God said that David was still good-looking. This confirms that no matter what you look like on the outside, if you have a relationship, the anointing of God in your life, a little dirt won't change a thing.

You may not have the best of clothes, or the best house to live in, or the fanciest car, but the anointing makes the difference. I find in my years with Christ that many of us stumble time after time with what God has called us to do because we feel we should have the same properties as the next man. This is not so, because there is a time and place for everything. Sometimes we have to do what God has called us to do first, even before we obtain the goods.

When David came into the room, this is when God spoke and said, "Yea, this is he to be the king." We can stand before the mirror and put on a ton of makeup, but it will accomplish nothing if we have not dealt with inner man. When others see the light of God radiating from us, it is the evidence of the anointing of God. When God anoints us, it causes everything to change in us and about us (1 Corinthians 5:17: "Therefore if any man be in Christ, he is a new creature: old things are passed away; behold all things become new"). When we allow the presence of God to rest in our lives, it really brings attention to us. This is why we need to be very careful concerning our actions—when we are in the public eye, especially. We are the only Christ some people will ever see. At some point, even the sinner man will stick his head in the tent door to get a glimpse of God's beauty, even if he doesn't stick around.

Let me share a story with you concerning this subject. When I was about twenty-five, I guess, a friend of mine invited me to his church because he was fond of me. At a certain part of the service, there was a woman standing and talking. I was not paying attention at one point, but as the voice began to elevate in praise, I noticed her in an undeniably supernatural light. At that very moment, I could not take my eyes off of her. I stared at her in amazement until she took her seat. As she approached her seat, she let out even more sounds of praise, and even the more she was interesting to me. At that moment, I told God in my heart that whatever she had, I wanted it. I did not know why, but I had to have what she had. The woman was so beautiful with the beauty of holiness, and I felt like I could not do without it in my life. Yes, she had beautiful skin and long black hair, and she was lean, but there was something beyond her beauty that attracted me to her. I was a Christian, but noticing her reflected just how much more of God I needed and wanted. Believe it or not, maybe about seven years or more, I saw that same woman at the post office and was able to let her know how much of an impact she had made in my life just by looking at her and seeing what I did not know at the time was God's glory residing in her. She thanked me for approaching her, and the words came at a good time, because she had just lost her husband, and she need to hear something positive. We may not see what others see in us because it is supernatural, and we cannot always see the supernatural. It behooves us to get in the presence of God and allow God to display his beauty. Our beauty should not be contingent upon what bottle of makeup we choose the length of our hair, the size of our breasts, or the color of our eyes. It is nice to have confidence, but it is even better to have evidence, evidence that the God we serve has influenced us enough to make a change in not only our lives but the lives of others. The inner beauties we possess are the only things that will get us from earth to glory.

David was never named king because of what he looked like. His kingship was based upon his heroic acts, obedience, and love for God, just to name a few. When God chooses, he takes what he can use for and in his kingdom. God is interested in using us as a holy vessel. Therefore, God needs to be the one behind the scenes, doing our makeup. When the curtains come up, it needs to be all God. God needs a yielded vessel to show his power to the world. Ladies, if we are depending on lips, hips, and fingertips to get us where we need to be, we are in for a rude awakening. The only kind of woman that uses these things to obtain favor and prestige is an escort.

CHAPTER THREE:

Beauty vs. Glory

We as Christian women of God should rely on God's glory, not faded glory. By "faded glory" I am referring to the beauty that glows only as long as the cosmetics are applied. I am talking about the beauty that washes off when the water or makeup remover comes in contact with it. The beauty we possess should come from the God-given heart and the spirit he has endowed us with to live as Christians. If outer appearance was the only thing we had going for us, we all would be in woe several years down the road. At some point in time, gravity begins to work against us, no matter who we are or how beautiful we think we are.

Some of us may say, "I still look good, even at the old age I have become." It could very well be true, but can you still attract what you attracted years ago, and can you get a prayer through and reach God? Can you intercede for your brother or sister and get a response from God? Can you discern who and what is around you? If and when we look to outer beauty to get us through life, what happens when the aging process really overshadows us? When our eyes grow dim, our breasts sag, our hair becomes thin, our buttocks drop, and our teeth take a swim every night, how will we be able to obtain what we need if we have always relied on our outer beauty? These insecurities are why some of us go to the doctor to get shot in the face with a needle. What has become of this world today, and why are we so hooked on appearance? This is why: the world has told us for so long that we have to look like or be the same size as a celebrity or we don't fit. One of the most important things in the world are making sure we are healthy on the inside, spiritually and naturally.

CHAPTER FOUR:

What's Eating You?

Did you know a blemish that appears on the outside of our skin sometimes tells us that there is something on the inside of us out of sync? We may never get to the bottom of every cause, but it's true. Many times, we think we have our expressions in control and no one can tell what is in our hearts, but whatever is on the inside shows on the outside.

For instance, we eat something that we don't know we are allergic to. What is the first thing that happens? Our skin breaks out in small blisters or rashes. This indicates that our bodies disagree with what we have put in our bodies. The same is true in the spirit realm: as we entertain different entities not of Christ, it will show up on the outside in our lives. Sometimes we may think we have some dysfunctions covered, but it shows on the outside This is why we must be careful as to what we eat spiritually, because it will show up in our carnal man.

In the natural, people are interested in diamonds and rubies, not stones and rocks. If we are going to be effective, the same is required in the spirit realm. If we operate out of cosmetics, there is no way we can be effective in the spiritual kingdom of God. Many times, this is why we are defeated—because we are trying to operate out of the spirit of God illegally. What I mean is that in order to operate out of the spirit of God, there has to be some God in us. We can't operate a machine we don't have a license for, and if so, we are in violation. This is why the seven sons of Sceva were whipped—because they were in violation (Acts 19:13–16). In some instances and some occasions, we ask God for a number of favors. He tells us to ask what we may, and he will give it to us. Nevertheless, it does not give us a license to freestyle in this walk with him. We must come into a covenant relationship with God. This is the only way we are going to get the full benefits of what he has promised us. I don't know about you, but I want all God has for me, and if I don't get it when I ask, I don't want it to be because I have stagnantly missed the mark.

When it is all about us, there is no room to service anyone else. It becomes 90 percent you and 10 percent God. We must be careful as to where we are entrusting our beauty to lie. The inner beauty is what causes us to walk in the awesomeness of God. The inner beauty sanctions us to operate in the anointing God has bestowed upon us. When we operate in the beauty of holiness, we can live according to God's plan and never have the burden of not possessing the power and promises of God. God is not impressed by numerous kinds of makeup. Beauty is a mind thing, but a beautiful thing when we have the mind of Christ. God does not need another pretty face to carry out his plan—in fact, that is the last thing he needs. God knows that when we operate out of vainglory, the truth is far from us.

CHAPTER FIVE:

Chosen for Greatness

When God chooses someone to carry out his will, he has already issued a background check. God already knows what we have been through, who we have been with, what we have been with, and what we did when we were with it. We can never hide it from God, no matter how prudish we try to be. He knows we have been hurt, who hurt us, and how bad they hurt us. He knows who we have hurt and how bad we hurt them, and the list goes on. Therefore, nothing takes God by surprise, but it does not exempt us from obtaining his glory. We are forgiven vessels. Therefore, when we allow God to caress us with his glory, we are then fit for the master's use. Don't allow anyone to deceive you into thinking that God cannot use you because of your history. God does not need to do a credit check on you to use you.

God already knew David's heart and his capabilities. God was fully aware of David's issues in his life that needed to be dealt with, but he was chosen anyway. No matter what you have dealt with or are dealing with now, don't get it twisted—God can still use you as long as your heart is in the right place. Go ahead; use all the makeup you want, just never forget about your heart. 1 Samuel 16:7 says, "...for the Lord sees not as man sees; for man looks at the outward appearance, but the Lord looks on the heart."

David was already in preparation when he was called out as king. He was in the field getting ready for the big fight that he knew nothing about. I am sure that just like I have, many of you have been in some hot, sweaty, nasty, stinky places that you just wanted to get out of but were forced to stay in, only to see later that it was for the sake of your ministry and the anointing.

There were several applications denied before Samuel found the right king. I can imagine Samuel from a twentieth-century standpoint, giving God several background reports. As God inspects each one, he throws them out, saying "No, no, no, no, and no" until he gets to David's. God told Samuel he was looking for a specific person to award the title of king. After passing all of David's brothers before him, when he got to David, I can imagine David's resume stating, "David is a warrior—check. David praises—check. David is a protector—check. David is a hard worker—check. David is a man after God's heart—check, check, and check." Now Samuel has realized he has God's man in view. Let's not forget, God also knew David was a womanizer, murderer, and cheater, but it was his heart and willingness to operate out of the spirit of God that landed him the position of king. The title of king or queen was not something that just anyone was chosen to possess. We have to meet special requirements before we can take office. We have to be like David; although he was a good-looking young man, he also had his priorities in check. David spent quality time with God and sang praises unto him, and in spite of his shortcomings, he was honest with God. There is no place of carnality in the kingdom. Saul was a coward and a lover of possessions and couldn't follow instructions.

When God said, "Not this one," he was saying no to someone who had a tall statute, who was pretty, smart, rich, etc. Ladies, God is looking for someone who is not afraid to break a nail. He can't use someone who can't go unless they have new clothes. God is looking to use someone who will go with the old clothes they have had for the last four years, because they know it is not about the clothes, it's about the kingdom. When David went against Goliath and was offered armor to wear, David refused, because he already had what it took to win the battle. We have to know that God has already given us what we need for battle, and it's not in a bottle. We just have to say no to false securities that we have smeared our lives with. We have to be original when it comes to the workings of God. The originality I am talking about is the gifts and anointing God has given us as individuals. When God chooses leaders, God chooses someone who doesn't think or know that he/she is the smartest kid on the block. I have done my best ministry in dummy-mode, meaning that God has used me on impulse to minister to others, and I had no idea what I was going to say to a confused or hurting person. The reason I was able to minister to that hurting person was because at one point, I was in their place of hurt. I gave up trying to look cute to be noticed and got serious with God.

God won't use our glitz and glamour because he is the only one who is allowed to shine. God want others to know that when situations are worked out in our lives, it is him that is responsible for it and not man. He wants others to know he is the God of "yea" and "amen" when we follow his ordinances. He needs the world to know it was not our looks that got us where we are today and that our outer appearance had nothing to do with the anointing in our lives.

By the way, the anointing in our lives actually comes from the not-so-pretty things that occur on a daily basis, minute to minute, hour to hour, day to day, year to year, and circumstance to circumstance in our lives. God wants others to know it was not our outer appearance that brought the miracles about. It is important to know it was not where we lived that drew others to Christ. It is necessary that the world knows that although our weave was tight, it had nothing to do with our success in God. It does not impress God that our tops are cut low or our dresses are halfway up our thighs. Those distractions are for the carnal man and have no place in the kingdom of God. Therefore, it should not be named among us. On that note, if we want to impress a good man, then modesty is the avenue we need to take. Allow that man to see the God in you, not the goods in you. The goods in you can take a turn for the worst at any time, because there is no good thing in us if we leave God out of it, and ladies, when we cover our goods, then that's when they become good.

I am sure some of the miracles we desire to see have not happened because we are too cute and not totally connected to the right source. How can God show us anything when we are in the mirror 80 percent of the time, checking our faded glory? What I mean by this is we sometimes as cutie pies don't want to get down and dirty when it comes to receiving greatness from God. We don't want to mess up our hair and nails and makeup to obtain help for others. We will get on our knees, but we won't stay long enough to hear what God has to say. We are too afraid we are going to mess up our expensive new clothes. We will go to prayer meetings, but we won't tarry, because our makeup may run. These are reasons why deliverance cannot take place—because we are too cute. We refuse to dance before the Lord, because we are afraid a strand of hair will come out of place.

I remember one Sunday I had put on makeup just to change up a little from the old me. Early in the service, during worship, I felt the spirit moving on me. I wanted to let go and allow God to do what he was attempting to do, but I thought about how the mascara was not waterproof. So what I did was quench the spirit, because I did not want to look like a raccoon when the tears stopped flowing. After that Sunday, I said I will never wear makeup again to church, because it robbed me of whatever deliverance I was going to receive. Whatever our holdup is, it is imperative we get rid of it. The very hindrance we allow to keep us from our miracle is what we need to get rid of, whether it is in us or on us. God wants others to know that miracles happen because of his power, not ours. God gave us outer beauty, but it is not to be compared to the beauty of holiness, sanctification, righteousness, and all that associates itself with his deity.

There is nothing wrong with putting a little paint on the barn or replacing the roof, but will it change the stance of the barn if it is not erected with the precise equipment? Will it stand when unfavorable weather conditions come? When the wind blows and the rain falls in our lives, will we be able to withstand the test of trials? Are we cute enough to withstand all of the trials and tribulations life will throw at us? If we don't have that inner beauty, we don't have strength, and when we don't have strength, we don't have joy, and when we don't have joy, we are a bunch of sad, mad, and hateful Christians. We may think at times when all is good that we are strong and can get through, but God has a tester.

CHAPTER SIX:

Fixed in the Valley

Job had what it took on the inside to get through a rough time in his life. Although he let a few degrading words about himself come out of his heart, he still stood and charged God, not foolishly. Job's possessions did not define who he was in God. When all is well, all is well. When all is wrong, all is wrong, no matter what we look like. We need more than beauty to go through these rough times in our life.

My appearance did not get me through the roughest valley I had ever been through some years ago; it was what God had instilled in me over the years. It did not matter that I had the best makeup money could buy. It was irrelevant that I had a beautiful car everyone would look at approaching the stoplight. It was totally out of the question that there were people I met along the way that totally loved me, or that I had a big family, because most of them thought I was strange anyway. What I needed was more of that inner beauty so I could have strength and joy. I needed something that would carry me when I said I was giving up. I needed something that would talk me down off of my spiritual ledge, and that was hope. I needed a source that would redirect me from the crucial mistakes in my life, and that was strength.

To have beauty is to have strength. I never knew how unattractive I could be until I went in the valley and came out. The valley has a way of putting a mirror in front of us to show who we are and who we are not. As long as I was on the mountaintop, I was a mess, because I depended on what I had or thought I had. We never really come to the knowledge of what we have until it is tried in the fire. The valley reflected avenues of corruption in my life I never knew were there. It was not that I did so much wrong, because I thought I was all right in my doings toward God.

There were many things that needed to be repositioned in my life. As I went through the valley, stopped in the valley, cried in the valley, became confused in the valley, threatened to give up in the valley, got mad in the valley, lost faith in the valley, wanted to die in the valley, but eventually transformed in the valley, God showed me what true beauty was. God showed me that true beauty was not what I possessed—it was when I possessed.

We can never really possess anything until we go through for it. The only way I can see us getting it is when we allow God to do our makeup. God sat me down at the edge of the banks during this process and talked to me like a father about his facts of life. He showed me that the true facts of life were from the inside.

True beauty is factual, because it illuminates all areas in our lives. God showed me what it took to obtain beauty. The valley is the place where I obtained many spiritual instruments needed in life, even for this book. Because of the valley, I am able to let the glory of God shine in my life for the purpose of saving souls, setting free the captive, and deliverance. When the works and trials of God come and we have no substantial evidence of God's beauty, we find ourselves in a mirror—not to prim and prance but to wipe the makeup our tears has washed down our faces, inquiring of God the turmoil in our lives. When we inquire of God concerning our circumstances, God may tell us that there is no circumstantial evidence of beauty in our lives. Therefore, we have to allow God to give us a makeover. There is one thing we must remember, and that is that we have to come to the full knowledge that God knows what he is doing.

When we sit at the beauty counters and they tell us what they are going to do about our uneven skin tone and fine lines, we don't fuss about it. We allow them to take whatever measures they need to take to make us flawless. On the other hand, when God attempts to give us a makeover, let us also be in agreement, because he knows what we need better than anyone else does. He knows all of our imperfections and knows what applications are needed to fix it. Let's not pretend that God does not know what we need.

In many instances, God attempts to makeover an area in our lives, but we refuse to allow him because we have become so immune to these dysfunctions. What we don't realize is that these are the very entities that are causing our uneven spiritual skin tone. We are shady and don't even realize it. We walk around thinking no one can see that our foundation has two shades. Holding on to what we think we need is like having on two different shades of makeup, because we are operating out of our old man and telling a new man lie out of our mouth. The newness of God is the beauty of God. We should never allow compliments of others to fool us into thinking that we are OK. There is an old saying that I am sure many of you have heard people say: "Beauty is only skin deep." Beauty goes past the skin; beauty is soul and spirit deep. If we don't have the right spirit about God's matters, it is null and void. And if our soul and spirit is not right, we are in a terrible mess. The most beautiful union in the world is when our spirit and soul come to an agreement, and we become what God has called us to be.

I never really knew the depth of doing something halfhearted until sometime ago. I realized that if our heart is not right in what we do, then it is halfhearted. I hear some people say—and I have said this myself—"I am doing a certain thing because I am supposed to." I did not do it because it was in my heart to do.

Back in the day, when our mom would ask something of us to do for her, as kids, sometimes we wouldn't be so pleased at all. Oftentimes, because we had been outside playing all day and were tired and lazy, we showed expressions of regret when the command was given. Therefore, because of the response we showed, she would stop us in our tracks and say, "Never mind, I will do it myself. Get out of here!" If we perform tasks out of our soul and leave our spirit out, then whatever we do is incomplete. There must be a balance in our lives or else we will live an unfulfilled life. Our soul man functions out of our emotions; our spirit man functions out of heaven. The soul man is mindful of the matters of the flesh, but the spirit man responds to the matters of God. Therefore, because we are human-soul beings, we tend to operate out of carnality. Therefore, because of this reason, the enemy of God attempts to lure us into this outer beauty pageant. No matter how many times others try to convince us that outer beauty serves every purpose, don't believe it; it's a lie from the bottom of hell. These are lies the enemy sends to attempt to deter us from the original plan of God.

Nothing has changed from the beginning of time in the garden, and let's not forget who the devil spoke with first. It's time to shut the mouth of the enemy once and for all. The beauty pageant he tries to position us in is the ultimate conduit to separation from God. Not only does it separate us from others, but it also separates our spirit man and causes us to operate out of carnality.

The deceiver uses this because the beauty we rely on and think we have will cause us to think we are better than the next individual. This is what the enemy wants, and his tactic is to isolate. This is the first step of destruction. The devil's game is to divide and conquer. He calculates that if he can get us to focus on our outer appearance, it will take our focus from what God really has planned for us. The devil knows that if he can get his voice in our ear canal, he can lure us into whatever avenue he wants. It is sad to say that many of us have heeded to the voice of the almighty deceiver concerning our outer beauty.

How do we know we have fallen prey to the voice of Satan? We focus more on the bottle of foundation than we do our spiritual foundation. We become more concerned about what shade of eye shadow to use rather than keeping our eyes on the prize. Many of us will not go out of the house if we don't have our makeup applied to our skin. But what about having the Word applied to our life? We need to have spiritual makeup applied to our life so that when we walk out, others can see that our spiritual foundation is made up of brick rather than straw, and just any gust of wind won't be able to huff and puff and blow our house down.

Others need to see that we are built upon a solid foundation, and nothing can move us. The most beautiful women in the world are the most powerful women, whether they are made up or not. Whether we realize it or not, others are looking for someone who can lead them on a straight path.

CHAPTER SEVEN:

A New Creature

Not every person who has not accepted Christ in their life desires to stay that way. There are others out there who desire to see what God has to offer, but many times, we are a stumbling block because of our actions. At some point in our lives, we fail to build our life on truth, which are the truths of God. There are so many obstacles to stand in our way of being what God has truly called us to be, ladies.

When we confess Jesus then walk contrary, we may as well put up a roadblock for the sinner man at the gates of heaven, because our actions determine their response to God 90 percent of the time. We must keep in mind that many people will never enter a church, so the church has to be in us, or we have to be the church. Women, don't forget, we are one of the most influential creatures on this earth, so let's make it positive. When we can blink our eyes and wiggle our hips to get a man to notice us, why not do something positive to get the world to see God? It does not take much; we must live according to the word of God.

In other words, we must live the inside-out life. When we permit God to live on the inside of us, it will truly show on the outside. When I first started attending a certain church, I thought I had to have something new every time I entered the doors, or at least not wear the same thing so close together.

If I didn't have something new, I felt constrained by the thoughts of the people, because the church I was attending at the time was about fashion, as I could see with my eyes. They had the shoe to match the purse and the jewelry, the hats to top off the outfit, and so forth and so on, and there is nothing wrong with that.

At one point, it stopped me from getting where I needed to be in God. I saw the well-dressed people dancing, singing, and seemingly having a good time. At this point, the way I was feeling, I dare to get up and respond as they did, because I was out of uniform, so I thought. What I did not realize was that I was dressed appropriately because I was there for the purpose of learning about and then magnifying God. Not to say that others weren't, it was just apparent that the dress code played a big part in most of the members' lives. In other words, when I did get to know them, God was not their priority. Some of their priorities were cheating, money laundering, home-wrecking, and backbiting, just to name a few. They were dressed up on their way to hell if they didn't get their priorities in check.

I felt a part as long as the jubilation was in process and no one was focusing on me, but as soon as it was over, I felt out of place, because it seemed everything they did was purely unofficial and cosmetic. I wanted more from God, but there was no one there that I could see to lead me to where I was trying to get to, even the pastor. They looked at me from head to toe as if to size me up in their minds with their shifty eyes. I would have stopped attending, but I knew this was where God wanted me to be, because there were a few things God wanted to show me and some facts he wanted to show them. Therefore, out of obedience, I stayed there. Later, I realized there was nothing wrong with my clothes, although they were not new, but there was something wrong with their makeup. They were made up of selfishness, envy, judgments, jealousy, backbiting, and more. If I had let the stares (Satan's voice) deter me, I would never have grown to where I am now in the Lord. I thank God that I am not where I was before in him, but I am glad about where I am now. And surely I would not have written this book, because this book was birthed from a relationship with God.

We as Christians have more influence than we really know. Ladies, if you have already made up in your mind that your carnal makeup is all you need, then allow God to give you a makeover. Sit in his high chair and allow him to get rid of all your spiritual blemishes and fine lines that so easily taint our surfaced beauty. Allow him to use his makeup remover to remove those unwanted entities in your life. We must allow God to do away with old beauty essentials and adopt some new ones. 2 Corinthians 5:17 says, "Therefore if any man be in Christ, he is a new creature: old things are passed away; and behold all things become new." When we have the mind of Christ, all our other actions will eventually mirror those of Jesus Christ.

Part Two

CHAPTER ONE:

The Beast Within

No matter how beautiful we may be on the outside, there is always a beast that lurks around, waiting to manifest itself. We can dance, shout, sing, and even preach over it, but the truth of the matter is, it is imperative that we deal with it. In order to move forward in our lives, we must make sure that the beast we have is put in its place, which is out of our lives. Time after time, we fail at one thing or another because we refuse to get rid of the beast that holds us hostage.

We as Christians may hate to admit it, but we all deal with one beast or another in our lives, whether it is jealousy, hatred, disbelief, unforgiveness, or whatever it may be. The truth is, we must deal with whatever our beast is so we can experience the domino effect of great exploits in our lives.

We attempt to operate in our ministry, work at our marriage, or even keep our families together but fail because we have not dealt with the beast within. Before we can move on with these concerns in life, we must first clear the path. We can decree and declare time after time in the name of Jesus, but some things in our lives need to be untangled so that our decrees and declares can manifest in our lives. If the sink is clogged with debris, then the water cannot flow through. The same is true for our lives when it comes to results. When we refuse to deal with our enemies, it causes many negative things to happen in our lives. We are taught that if we believe and have faith, those things will fall in line for us, and we will experience a prosperous life. But the truth is that it takes more than that. Yes, the bible is true; nevertheless, we need to demonstrate the whole bible, not what we agree with. We must dig in the Word to see what makes the decrees and declarations become effective. There are too many times we want what God has to offer, but we don't want to offer him anything. The promises of God require give and take. God told Abraham that he would make his name great, but Abraham had to be obedient to the instructions of God. Abraham was first called out from among familiarity, then he was given a promise, leading to a sacrifice of his son. The book of Deuteronomy, chapter twenty-eight, demonstrates the agreement between man and God. It is powerful, and I urge you to read it; it will bless your soul. When we give our lives to Jesus, there is an agreement between the two. The agreement is almost like a contract that we cannot break. If we break the contract, there will be repercussions. I ask, who would want to break a contract after reading Deuteronomy 28? There is promise and power in agreement.

CHAPTER TWO:

Stay Focused

When an airplane is destined to arrive at another location, it must be clear for takeoff. In order to decree anything, our lives must be clear so that the promises of God are "yea" and "amen." We cannot live any way we want and expect God to shower us with blessings.

When we decree and declare and believe God for our house, car, and money and it takes more time than expected, we get frustrated. We will sometimes get to the point of doubting God and threaten to do our own thing. The actuality is, sometimes there is an enemy that hinders the blessings and promises of God. Therefore, we need to examine to see what enemy is in our camp. When we find the hindrance in our lives and extract it, then we will be clear for takeoff to our destination. Many times, we are in denial that there is an enemy in our camp, because we are the pastor's son or daughter. We are the prophets, apostles, teachers, and preachers, and there is no enemy in us. I have been a Christian for sixty years, and there could not possibly be an enemy in me. I am the first lady, and the enemy resides in everyone else and not me, because I am on display every

Sunday. These are the lies the devil will tell us, because he does not want to be detected. We all want God to move in our lives, but we first must deal with the enemy within.

The scripture says that when we were asleep, the enemy came in, sewed tares, and went his way (Matthew 13:25). Being asleep is when we feel that because of our positions, we are exempt from the snares of the enemy. We feel like we are MC Hammer…can't touch this. Consequently, the enemy will make a deposit and keep it moving. This is how it is possible that the enemy can come in on our territory and wreak havoc. So how it is possible that we can sing, dance, shout, and worship, and the enemy can come in and make a deposit?

The truth that is revealed to me is this: sleep is when we get so intertwined in the things of life and fail to lock our doors. Hence, the enemy sees an opening, and he sneaks in. He waits until we are distracted with the cares of this world, and then he sneaks in. The distraction that occurs is not always negative. We can be so involved with the matters of someone else's heart until we forget our own. We must be careful as to how we leave our doors open. We should never get so distracted, we lose sight of that enemy.

If we are not careful, the enemy will invade our house, full of his kind, waiting to destroy. He does not bring his family in all at once; he brings them one by one, or two by two. Once our house is full, he can have access to our minds, hearts, bodies, and soul, leaving us wondering why there is a dilemma in our lives and how it got that way. In this instance, it will sometimes cause us to give up on the dreams we were so determined to see.

If the enemy cannot be detected, then he won't have to worry about being exposed or expelled. When the enemy attempts to deceive, he sends a small portion of what he has in our souls. It's like little, small doses of poison he feeds us until we are spiritually dead. He makes what will kill us look like nothing. There are so many seemingly small things that have a dangerous undercurrent. Nevertheless, if we are aware of these currents, we won't get sucked in.

CHAPTER THREE:

Unwanted Fruit

There are so many stems of chaos that come from one source. Let's take the spirit that runs so rampant in our churches: the spirit of jealousy. It has many smooth ways to present itself so that it won't be detected or seems harmless. This is how the enemy can destroy so many of the saints of God in these last and evil days. To operate under the radar, the enemy may cause an individual who has the spirit of jealousy to act as if they are happy about what others are obtaining. In fact, the only reason they want to know everything in your business is because they don't want you to have more than they do, and they will want to know where you got it so they can get better.

Some people get pleasure out of staying on top of you. They always want you to stay close to them so they can know your every move. They are the first ones to declare they are happy for you but secretly want you to fail or not have more than they do. They always want to know every single detail in your life. They need to know what you bought and where you bought it from. They need to come over and see it, and later, they will have one just like it. I remember I had this friend who I thought was a true friend to me but was secretly jealous of me. She always acted like she wanted me to have the best; she would always voice that I deserved the best. At one point, I believed her, but God opened my eyes to who she really was. I was disappointed, but at the time, I had to rely on her for some necessities.

She was good, as long as I was depending on her for it. As long as she could know my every move, she was satisfied. She would pretend she was praying for me to get what I needed. I was going through a divorce, and my life had taken an unpleasant turn. I watched her time after time as she pretended to lie about how much she wanted me to have what I needed. One day, I made her think I was about to get what I needed, and I saw a look of panic on her face. This was when if I had any doubt about her not wanting me to have my own, it was gone that day. I was shocked and disappointed at the same time and a little angry. She had nice things and was almost out of debt, but she fell back into debt because she thought I was about to exceed what she had. I learned to be aware when some people say they are happy for you but secretly envy you. Sometimes when people bend over backwards for you, watch their motives!

Another enemy is the spirit of control. Example: when their idea is always better than someone else's idea and they want you to always do things their way. They manipulate you in a crafty way to get you to move in their direction. They know just what to say, how to say it, and when to say it to move you. If we are not careful, the enemy will suck our brain out of our heads with enticing, cunning words. This is also the first cousin to witchcraft. There are so many other mechanisms that stem from one sin. I am not ashamed about the confession I am about to make, hoping it will help someone.

I was in a situation with my late husband, and there was something he needed. The only way he could obtain it was with me. Of course, he had taken me through great trials, and I was almost fed up with him. I decided that because I was almost there with him, I was not going to oblige him, and I felt good about it too. On my way to work that morning, I went through my mind about how it wouldn't happen if I had to do it. As soon as I parked my car at work, the Lord scolded me and told me I controlled no one's destiny. Later, he revealed to me that I was operating in the spirit of witchcraft (control). I was so hurt about it; all I could do was cry. I was hurt because God was not pleased with me, and I was doing all I could to please God but was not aware that someone had invaded my territory. The reason the enemy was able to plant that seed was because I let what he was taking me through throw me off track. We must be so careful as to what vein we are operating out of. I let anger force me to a place I thought I never would be in. What leader or Christian wants to operate out of a foul spirit? These sightings are what we call undercurrents.

There are various undercurrents that go on to destroy us. I don't excuse the fact that this is something that happens, and sometimes it's not totally our fault. Some of us on a day-to-day basis have so much going on, such as ministering to others in hope and faith that they are established until we forget about ourselves. Some of us just lose focus because we are in other people's business, which should not be named among us. Either way, we should learn to take inventory of our lives on a day-to-day basis. We need to find out where our negative actions stem from and what the enemy has planted when we were asleep, wide awake.

We may go through life with people telling us that we have a certain forcefulness about us. We may not agree with them because the enemy has disguised the spirit of control deep within us. We should always be aware what has taken residence in our home so we can evict them and move on. For myself, when I am shown the truths, then I want to do the truth. Some things in our lives may take a little more time than others, but we must deal with it no matter how long it takes. We are not going to move forward in fullness until the beast is removed.

CHAPTER FOUR:

Kill the Beast

I know many of us has seen or heard of the famous cartoon *Beauty and the Beast* before. It's by far one of my favorites to watch. There are many reasons for me being interested in this movie, which I think will come out in this chapter. We all have a type of beauty, and we all have some type of beast we deal with from time to time. I love seeing how Belle's love brings the beast back to his original state. I also love when two people come together no matter what side of the track they come from. Despite their differences, love has a way of bringing them together.

Nevertheless, the beast I want to talk about is not some fairytale that is shown on television. The beast I am relating to is the beast within. Many of us will almost never admit that there is a beast inside of us that keeps us under the influence of defeat. Hundreds of times, we will dance, shout, and speak in tongues all over the beast within, because we never really want anyone to know what we are dealing with. The truth of the matter is, we need to deal with this beast in order to get positive results. Some of the reasons we don't see what God has promised is we are not in a place to receive, meaning we are not in the right postures to receive. Instead of dealing with the enemy within once and for all, we give the enemy a vacation, meaning we will put the enemy out then allow him to come back because the enemy has conned us into thinking we are empowered by our dysfunctions.

This beast will do everything to keep the beauty in us suppressed. His whole tactic is to keep us bound with the cares of this world. He does not want us to live the way God intended us to live. One hundred percent of the time, we need to deal with the beast within before the beauty can emerge. The beauty and the beast on the inside are constantly at war with each other. When certain circumstances occur in our lives, we want to display the beauty as a child of God, but the beast seems to get in the front seat first. The beast would love to think that he oversees, when in fact, if we resist the beast (devil), he will flee. The beast is constantly whispering to our minds wrongdoings to stagnate us. There is nothing too big or small that he won't attack concerning our lives. He wants nothing more than to keep us from reaching our assignments and destinies. He always finds pleasure in keeping our minds bothered, our hearts heavy, and our fears on blast. He would love nothing better than for us to give up on what God said we can have, especially those of us who have a "much is given, much is required" ministry assigned to our lives.

The enemy would be ecstatic to see us retreat to Egypt in our minds, hearts, and eventually, in our physical actions. Because his promised land is not like ours, he never wants us to enter our promised land. Before we can walk into total deliverance, we must bring this beast under subjection to the power of God. The word of God says that the fight we face is not carnal. We are not fighting flesh and blood when we can't seem to shake what is bothering us on the inside, or even with another individual.

When we were born, we were given an identity, which is a name. As we grew and were able to comprehend voices and thoughts, we responded to them. When someone called us, we answered to the voice and responded to the command. Therefore, it is imperative to have knowledge of what we are dealing with when it comes to the beast within. This is the only way we are going to rid ourselves of the beast and become free. If we never learn how to assess the problem, the enemy will have a field day with our minds. Not only once will he have a field, but he will continue repeatedly until he has completely stolen our minds. We as Christians operate in the flesh, but we should not try to war in the flesh, because the weapons of our warfare are not carnal. We are fighting against principalities of the air and the ruler of this earth. If I'm always getting angry at myself because I failed at something, I will always be defeated. I need to know what demon is keeping me from succeeding. There could be several elements that are keeping me from my post of succeeding.

There could be an element of fear, unforgiveness, rage, verbal abuse, physical abuse which causes anger, torment, and the list goes on. If I continue to look at the outward visual of my issues, I will be defeated every time. But when I go in the spirit realm to fight, then I win every time, because God teaches us how to be warriors. God gives us mighty weapons of war. God gives us access and power to fight the enemy of our minds (2 Corinthians 10:3–6).

God gives us the power to pull down strongholds in our lives. Strongholds are those things in our lives that keep us going back to the alter time after time for the same thing. In simple form, it's those chains that keep us in bondage. We know all too well who is behind these things. In my life, I found that many of us have the tendency to turn from what we really need to deal with. We feel if no one knows the beast we hide on the inside, then we don't have to deal with it. However, if we don't deal with the beast, it's going to deal with us.

When problems arise in our lives and we have not dealt with the beast that triggers the emotion, he will demonstrate his residency in our being. How much turmoil will we allow to wreak havoc in our lives until we do something about it? We should be like the lady with the issue of blood when she was determined that she would get the touch she needed to be healed of her issues.

Countless times, we don't want to deal with our issues, and sometimes we don't know how. What we must do is be willing to admit the beast we are dealing with then allow God to address the issue. There are some beasts we deal with that only God can handle, but we need to confess that we need help. The sooner we deal with what is eating us, the sooner we will walk in deliverance. When I say eating us, I mean it is literally eating away at heart, mind, and soul, then after, the spirit follows. The reason it's hard for some of us to operate out of the spirit is because we have been eaten alive. Not dealing with our issues is very detrimental and will at some point destroy us. No matter what issue we have in our flesh, there is nothing God can't deliver us from, but we must be willing to let it go.

We cannot continue to hold on to something that will eventually cost us everything. I realized some time ago that in order to gain, we must lose. When I lose the sin, I gain power. Many times, we get a grip of something and refuse to let it go, because the enemy has convinced us that this thing is what we need to make it. There are many things in life we will have to let go of, and sometimes it is the very thing we love. Again, I realized that whatever has been taken, God has a better replacement. We need to just trust God to do what he is going to do in our lives. It may be hard, but if we trust him, he will prove himself.

In different situations, I noticed we hold on to the beast in our lives because we feel comfortable, because it gives us fabricated power we feel we can hide behind. When the words of God said, "Come out from among them and be ye separate," it was not only talking about the natural things; it was certainly talking about those spiritual entities also. It is not so hard at times to walk away from the physical things, but in the spiritual, there lies a challenge. The reason for such a challenge is the mind never leaves us. The mind is where our every concern is stored. Therefore, it is imperative that we are mindful as to who is controlling our minds. When we allow God to take charge of our lives, we walk away from all dysfunctions of life.

For instance, if we have been hurt in a relationship once or twice, we have the tendency not to give all our heart to the other person we may be involved with, not realizing that we are being unfair to the other individual because they are giving their all, or we won't trust an honest person because of our past experiences. The thing we fail to realize is that we are operating out of a spirit of judgment. We judge the person before we really get to know them, and these actions leave room for an early-onset dysfunctional relationship. When we push away genuine actions from others, it causes us to miss out on greater love. I found that a great number of relationships never work because we take our dysfunctions to their dysfunctions, and no one is ever happy. Often, we find ourselves just existing in a relationship, never really getting full benefits from it.

When we invest in something, we want full benefits from it; therefore, we must be willing to give our all. We must allow God to deal with the issues in our life so we can walk in wholeness. When we decide to accept true love from others, let's make sure we can give it back. Don't expect to receive and not be willing to give. It does not work this way. Let's stop the beast from snatching from us as soon as we get ready to receive the riches God has prepared for us. Fear gets in the way and paralyzes us when something God has sent seems too good to be true. We want to embrace the things of God, but we allow the enemy to come in and not only take a front seat but drive for us. Therefore, he drives us right off the cliff to a spiritual death. It is necessary that we trust God in every aspect of our lives, no matter how difficult it may be. He is God, he knows what he is always doing, and nothing catches him by surprise.

CHAPTER FIVE:

Let Go and Let God

Trying to control our lives so that incidents won't happen to us again is a plane crash ready to happen. We need to take control of that beast by the neck and suffocate it. In essence, what we are really saying is that we don't trust God to work certain situations out in our lives. If we trust God with all, then we would know that God will not let us get into something that will permanently damage us. He might take us through a trial but never permanently hurt. If God be for us, then who can be against us? Anyone can be against us, but no weapon that is set out to hurt us will do us any harm ever.

I remember in my marriage, when it began to take a turn for the worse, I panicked and started putting up a shield around myself. I was so devastated, because I had given it all I had, and it didn't seem to change. I did not want to look like a fool before people and my family, because people are quick to judge. In my mind, I thought I was blissful the first few years in my marriage, and because my husband started to take me for granted and thought it was all right to do so, I had secret thoughts about how I could stop him or how I could shield myself. I started to withdraw my loving actions toward him little by little. It got to the point where it started to toy with my emotions, because I still loved him very much, but I felt like I should control myself. I was getting distracted from what I needed to do and could not stay focused, because I would always ponder about the outcome of the marriage and my image. I could not bear to have a failed marriage when we had been so happy once before. I was talking to my best friend Katrina Blount one day about how I was feeling about the issue in my marriage as I had once before, and out of the blue, she said, "Dorothy, God said trust him with you." At that very moment, there was a feeling of relief, because my Father was telling me, "My sweet baby, I got you; don't worry, because all of this is going to turn out for your good." God used my best friend to come and kill that beast that was taunting me day after day, as the Philistine did the people of God.

Did you know that fear is a very common and natural thing to us, but it can easily turn our lives into a living hell? Everything that has fear stamped on it is a sure failure. Fear stops us from doing any and everything we need to do for God.

When I was called to the ministry, I was very afraid, and the fears almost paralyzed me. The last thing I wanted to do was get in front of people to speak. The devil would defeat me in my mind before I could even start to think what it would be like. He would whisper so many things to me about what the people would think, how not ready I was, and how others would look at me. He had a field day with my mind and caused me to become stagnate for some time. Nevertheless, the more I got acquainted with God, the closer I came to doing what God had ordained me to do. As long as I listened to him, I was defeated and would never obtain the blessings that are yea and amen from God. I finally made up in my mind that I would not allow him to keep me in bondage anymore concerning this. This is just one of the fiery darts he will throw at us, but it is a major one.

There is power given to us to shut the mouth of the enemy, and that is the word of God. The word of God becomes a weapon when we use it. The word of God has the solution to every problem we encounter. When the devil attempted to make Jesus command the stones to be made bread, Jesus gave him the Word. Jesus told him natural bread sustains but for so long. In essence, he was saying that the bread of life was that of importance. When the devil showed Jesus kingdoms and offered him power, Jesus rebuked him.

Again, the Lord was saying that there is only one God to worship, and that is the creator of the universe—then there was the last attempt on the knowledge of God. The devil told Jesus to jump and let the angels catch him; the Word said, "He will give his angels charge over you." Then Jesus said to the devil, "You shall not tempt the Lord." (Luke 4:3–12) In essence, Jesus was saying, "You have no idea who you are dealing with, Satan; get lost." You see, when we give the devil the Word enough to let him know we believe the Word, he will flee from us. This is what I had to do when he attacked my mind with the fear of doing the will of God. I had to show the devil better than I could tell him that I had a greater on my side. I was determined to do the will of God because of my relationship with him.

To make that long story short, I am now walking in authority of God because I chose to shut the mouth of the enemy. You ever heard the phrase, "Never let them see you sweat"? When we don't respond to what he throws at us, he can never really know what our weaknesses are. Let me take you another route: resist the devil, and he will flee.

When we announce that we are children of God, we should be at our best at removing anything that is not like God from our lives. It is easy to walk away from people that are not like God, but it can be very difficult to expel those imperfections from our beings. Many times, people will say that the closest one to us is the one we fall prey to and that they can hurt us. But the beast on the inside is the one that will and can destroy us if we allow it to. We eat with it, sleep with it, and talk with it every day. We should work toward perfection each and every day. We should be pressing toward a higher calling each and every day. The higher callings are peace, love, trust, kindness, wisdom, knowledge, and understanding on a whole new level; this is the beauty against the beast we deal with on a daily basis. When someone is in a race and jumps one hurdle, they don't stop at one—they brace themselves for the next one. The race is never over until all hurdles are cleared.

Therefore, when we clear our hearts and minds from one entity, we brace ourselves for the next one. Because the beast has so many faces and comes in many forms, there will always be something we will have to deal with. Nevertheless, we should constantly keep our minds steadfast on the things of God (Luke 11:24). "When the unclean spirit is gone out of a man, he walks through dry places, seeking rest; and finding none, he said, I will return into my house where I came out of."

Therefore, when we have rid ourselves of one beast, quickly shut and lock that door! If we lock the door behind them, stand ready to receive the greater infillings of the Holy Spirit. Remember, when he comes to knock on your door again, he's bringing company, but if we are filled, then there will be no room for him or his cousins. The old man should never be allowed to take up residence in our lives as he did before. When the old man tries to come back in our lives, we should respond the way our body does when we eat something that does not agree with it: throw it back up. In Ephesians 4:20–24, Paul tells the Ephesians to put off the old, corrupted man (beast) that caused deceitful lust in their beings. Then he tells them to be renewed in the spirit of their minds. Afterward, he goes a little further to say, "Put on the new man (beauty)." That new man Paul is talking about is the beauty of holiness and righteousness of God.

Therefore, when those foreign entities start to wake up for attention, we can cast them down and throw them out. When they arise, we should speak the same words of Jesus when the devil tried to tempt him: "Satan, get behind me." We will never walk in freedom until we identify what beast torments and then cast him out. Sometimes it is hard to see the enemy for what it really is because it can camouflage itself so well. What we think is innocent and can cause no harm could be the very thing that takes us down.

CHAPTER SIX:

Resist, Refuse, and Revoke

Let's take flirting, for instance, ladies—something we are good at. No good woman or man intends to cheat on their spouse, right? OK, just say we feel flirting is no big deal and we do it sometimes. If we do flirt, it may seem innocent enough. What we don't realize is that we are cheating on a low level, sending mixed signals to the other individual. The enemy then has us under the radar with our thinking. He has deceived us into thinking that it's OK, but it's not.

Before I go any further, there will always be someone out there who has something more attractive than your spouse. No matter how much we love our spouse, they don't have everything we could ever want, because they are not perfect. Therefore, we love them because they have enough for us to overlook what we can live with, because what God has put together, let no man separate.

The imperfections we have do not in any way give permission to the devil to trick us into thinking it's alright to flirt. When we allow the enemy to trick us into this seemingly innocent act, it will come back to bite us. Playing the game of the enemy will cost us in the long run.

Things may be good at home if we decide to flirt, but what if at some point there is a bump in the road in the marriage? The first thing the enemy will do is ask for his pay by reminding you of how Suzy or John looked at you in a way you have never been looked at before when you were flirting with them. What do we do now? Do we act on that incident, or do we erase it from our minds? Some of us, not knowing or thinking about what is going on, will take that innocent flirting to another level. The enemy will take our strongest areas and stop at nothing to diminish them with his tactics. We have to be like Jesus and resist the devil, and he will flee from us.

In the garden of Eden, the enemy used the desire to be wise and powerful against Adam and Eve. Look at what he said in Genesis 3:5: "For God knows that in the day you eat of the tree, your eyes shall be opened, and you shall be as gods, knowing all things." The enemy also lied to them concerning their demise after eating of the tree. In verse four, he told them they would not die after God clearly said they would. What the enemy did was bring the two down to his level to start the mind process of never having to die. The beast is what always walks contrary to the word of God. Again, Ephesians 4:31 tells all of the beast we have to deal with on a daily basis. There is no beast bigger or less dangerous than the other. If we let the small snake stay around, he will eventually grow. When we allow the enemy to stay around us, we become tempted to go back to the old mess again.

This is why when I have a taste for chocolate cake, I have to buy only a couple pieces, so I won't be tempted to eat a whole cake in a short period of time. Every time we succumb to the enemy, we are giving him power over us. Oftentimes, we wonder what happened in our lives concerning certain situations. We even ask sometimes, "How in the world did this happen, and how did I get here?" Matthew 13:25 said, "But while men slept, his enemy came and sowed tares among the wheat, and went his way." This is why it's important to know what we possess that the enemy is after.

Never be ignorant of the devices of the enemy. Stop sleeping on what we are supposed to be doing in the kingdom of God. Wake up to what God is calling you to. After we discover what the enemy is after, then we need to do all we can to protect it. Being saved is not just professing; it is to possess the righteousness of God. Sin has no place in heaven and should never have a place in our lives. Without holiness, no man shall see God. We have to stop being comfortable with our lives, because this is when the enemy comes in to sow the tare. In other words, we need to come out and stay out of sleep mode.

When I was younger, I was a daydreamer. One of my siblings would catch me daydreaming and throw a ball at me and simultaneously say, "Think fast!" If I did not come out of my daze fast enough, the ball would hit me in the face, stomach, or wherever the ball was aimed. This is what happens when are asleep when we should be awake. The enemy doesn't announce—he just pounces.

Sometimes the enemy will come so sudden and fast, we don't have enough time to regroup or even reposition ourselves. It's a bad feeling to get the wind knocked out of us, and there is nothing we can do about it. I have missed and slept on so many opportunities in my life, but I refused to let many more get past me. I am determined to redeem the time lost and walk in victory. Not only am I ready, but I also want my brothers and sisters in Christ walking in the same victory.

Part Three

CHAPTER ONE:

The Queen in You

Ladies, did you know that there is a queen in every woman who allows Christ to reside in her life? No matter how tainted we think we are because of life's circumstances, there is a queen in us. Although we have encountered many hurtful things and have threatened many times to give up hope, we must know that we are still the queens of the world. There have been and for some still are frustrations that have pushed their way into our lives to deter us from acknowledging the truth about ourselves. For some time now, the enemy has held a mirror of defeat to our faces, forcing us to believe the lies that have held us hostage for many years.

The enemies of rape, prostitution, drug addiction, alcohol abuse, incest, divorce, past homosexuality, rejection from family members, pregnancy out of wedlock, mental and verbal abuse, you name it could really play a great part of our shame and feelings of unworthiness in our lives. Although we may have encountered some or one of these hurts, it is imperative that we know that God will use that very hurt to help heal someone else.

You may ask yourself, "How could I possibly help someone in the situation that bends me over in pain?" Maybe at this time you are hurting yourself and feel this is not what you need to hear. Believe me, if you grab hold of who you are and what God has for you, it will change everything about you. God never intended for us to encounter many of these hurts, but because of our surroundings, we were and are exposed to these adversities. Many of us never asked to be in these places of frustration, but here we are. Nevertheless, no matter how we got there and no matter what we think about ourselves, there is a way out. Many of us focus so much on how we got into a situation, we forget how and who to ask for directions out of it.

When we make a conscious decision to live our life to the fullest with Jesus, all we were is cancelled out and all we have done is forgiven. We immediately stop being the victim and become women of victory. Ladies, we cannot let the enemy take our inheritance. When some of us think of inheritance, we think of money, but we as women of God have so much more to look forward to. There is an inheritance of respect, love, holiness, power, authority, hope, and the list goes on. It is important that we know what rightfully belongs to us.

We perish because we don't have knowledge of what belongs to us. An inheritance can be natural and spiritual, both belonging to us. Hebrews 11:8 states that Abraham was called to go into a place in which he would later receive an inheritance; this was the natural standpoint. 1 Peter 1:4–8 speaks about an incorruptible, undefiled inheritance that will never fade away, and that is the kingdom of God. No matter which inheritance it is, it belongs to us as children of God.

If we purchase an item from the store and we see that someone is trying to steal it from us, the first thing we do is make an approach, and women, you know how we can get when someone has trespassed on our property. The eyes glare the nose spreads, and that neck rolls like it has a pivot on it, and whoever is in violation will stop in their tracks. We need to have that same response when it comes to our inheritance that has been given to us. Being saved is part of our inheritance, and we need to protect it as if our life depends on it.

Actually, it does when we look at it from all angles. I feel that one of the reasons we are so depressed and double-minded is because the very thing we need to stay alive, we allow circumstance to take from us. We lie down and allow the "woe is me" to take over. What we don't realize is that when we receive the inheritance, we gain power. When there is power, there is deliverance, and when we are delivered, we move in the supernatural, causing signs, wonders, and miracles to take place. Let's cease from letting that past enemy creep in and out of our life, making us feel like a failure.

All trials and tribulations we go through in our lives should be a lesson learned whether it was planned or not. Nothing just happens to us, and there is a purpose for everything we've gone through, although some of it was of our own ignorance. We have sat at the gate as a leper, we have been at the gate called beautiful waiting for help, and we have been blind like Bartimaeus at Jericho, begging for help, and now is the time to take up our beds and walk.

Ecclesiastes 3:1 states: "To everything there is a season, and a time to every purpose under the heavens." We first have a purpose, then the set time comes to fulfill it. "Everything" in verse one means that every trial we have ever gone through or will go through is on a set schedule. We can go carefree in the world, and it will be our demise, but when we are purpose it changes the plan. When God allows a thing, it is to help, not to harm. The devil may mean it for our demise, but God turns it around according to how we handle the situation. As we know, during the four seasons, something unique and different takes place in each one.

In the spring, plants and flowers begin to blossom in an array of beautiful colors. In the summer, the temperature gets to its highest. In the fall, the tree leaves change colors and fall to the ground, introducing the coming winter months. In the winter months, much of the time, the snow and rain freezes, sometimes stopping most of our activities. The changing of seasons has to take place, so it is the same in our lives. In order for God to keep us moving, because he is a moving God, he has to create a season to show us where we are and to keep us on our spiritual toes. If we continued in one season all of our lives, we would never see the promises and inheritances of God as he promised. We would never be able to experience the different seasons of life.

Therefore, we would never be able to experience God in such ways as we have already. God wants to show himself to us on many occasions and levels. At one time in my life, I felt as though I was stuck spiritually, and we all have been there. I did not know what to do or where to go. I had no mentor to follow and no one to turn to. I was seeing God and confessing him in the same way over and over again.

One day, I overheard someone saying that there were many sides of God and never knew what that meant. I didn't know how to seek God that deep, so I asked God if I could see another side of him, not knowing there was such a thing. I couldn't even imagine how that would be possible. In showing me, I meant I had to experience something I had never experienced before. It was not preferable, but I had to experience it to see that side of God. After all I had to encounter, I still could not see what I asked until the season came. In order for me to get God to move on the promise, I had to be in the right season. I found out that when we ask God for something the answer is not no, sometimes we have to be prepared for what we ask for. When we ask God for something, he already knows whether it is good for us or not. This is why we should not get discouraged when the prayer is not answered right away. If we see no results in our prayers, we should be finding out what to do in between asking and receiving. If we don't find out, we will be accusing of God not hearing us or not to giving it to us. The reason some of us get discouraged and give up is because the promises of God never seem to come fast enough. Just like everything else, our blessings and prayers are set on a time schedule. We cannot rush God because he knows when to release the blessings and promises. Most of the time, we don't see them right away, because we are not spiritually mature enough to obtain them. OK, so when do we have to be mature enough to get a blessing? This may be the question some of you are asking now. Didn't the word say, "Ask and you shall receive"? Yes, this is what the bible said to us, but it has a time limit on it ("To a time to every purpose under the heaven." Ecclesiastes 3:1). What about having faith and believing that God will perform the miracles and blessings I have been waiting for? This is true as well, but it still has a timer on it. When we cook and our hands become full of things to do in the kitchen, we set certain items on a timer to ensure they won't overcook or to make sure we add something to them before they get done. When the timer goes off, we add or remove them from the stove. Why? Because now they're ready. This is the same scenario when it comes to our blessings; we have to be ready or in a position to receive what God has in store for us.

CHAPTER TWO:

Seasons

We must come to a state of maturity of heart, mind, and spirit that we may receive these things. Trials and tribulations bring about maturity to our lives, and the reason some of us have not matured is because we haven't passed the tests. In order to move in God, there are many trying situations that will come to pass. We don't immediately go from glory to glory; growth is a process. What you are going through now is a process that will get you to another level in God. Never mind that it is or is becoming difficult to bear—just inquire of God of the season you are in.

You may be in a winter season, attempting to operate in a summer season. If you are, then I am here to tell you now: it's not going to work. Nothing we hope for will come to us in an off-season. No matter how many times people stand a give a word to the church, that word may not belong to you at that time. Not to say it is not going to happen, but we need to remember there is a time for everything. That's why we get discouraged—because we try taking every word to heart that is spoken to the church.

No matter how many expectations we have from God, if it is not your time, it's not your time. This was a hard thing for me to grasp when I was expecting God's goodness. I was that kind of Christian that called God to the carpet when I was expecting something. I gave God back his word. I decreed and declared what would come to me. I stood on his promises, and nothing happened. When the word came forth in these services, they didn't say to us that maybe this particular word was not for everybody.

The word some of us teach is that you can have what you say, something we all want to hear when we need a fix. The preacher, prophet, and evangelist didn't tell us that we had to be processed. Some of us want to live like we please and decree and declare a thing and expect it to come to pass. If this is the case, then I declare you are wrong in your thinking.

We can't grab at every word that comes to the house, because we may not have matured enough to receive it. If God would allow every word we hear to come to pass immediately, it would be like giving a ten-year-old keys to a car. He would not only hurt or kill himself, but there could also be others in the path of destruction.

The reason some of our ministries never last or get off the ground is because we have not matured enough to operate in them. In life, there are tests we must take in order to get to our next level or receive the promises of God.

In school before we go to the next grade, there are a series of tests we must take first to ensure that we are indeed ready to move on. The teacher never passes us along until our grades are satisfactory. God does not pass us, either, until we have passed our test. God is going to make sure that when we are on the battlefield, we are equipped. The more tests we pass, the more God releases the promises, blessings, and miracles.

When God told Abram to move to another place, he not only wanted him to move, but it was also necessary that he moved. Where Abram was had become a place of no more, meaning his time was up and it was time for greater. His winter season was over; now, it was time for a fall and spring season, the fall season meaning a falling away from family, and the spring season meaning going forward into a land where God would change his name from Abram to Abraham. You see, we have to lighten the load sometimes when God is trying to take us to another place. We have to remove weights from our minds, hearts, and souls so God can use us. We have to become mature enough to let go and let God do whatever he needs to do in our lives, no matter how much it hurts. Some of us told God we wanted to be all we could be for him; now is the time of testing. Don't even think about it; it's too late to take it back now that the heat is turned on. Jesus said, "No man putting his hand to the plough and looking back is fit for the kingdom" (Luke 9:62).

CHAPTER THREE:

Timing

If we are trying to operate in the wrong season, God cannot bless us the way he desires to. Never think for one minute that God is playing games with us by getting us to jump through hoops to be blessed. He is eager to bless his children with what we not only need but also want. Nonetheless, we have to be in a place to provoke him to do so. As God would mature me in areas, I would get very discouraged with my life. I would believe God for this, that, and the other, and it never seemed to reach me. Each time I would be in a church service and the speaker would speak something pertaining to what God said I could have, I would get excited. Later, when it did not come to pass, I would get annoyed and stop believing. I even tried to talk myself out of what God said I could have because I thought it would never happen for me. I thought in my immature mind that only certain people get those kinds of blessings. I would look at others in disbelief and resentment because they were getting what God said I could have. I would even question the man or woman of God that brought the word to the church.

I believed what the bible said about what I could have but forgot about the part where it said, "Wait on the Lord and be of good courage; there is a time for everything; stand; thou it tarry, wait on it." These are the truths I failed to remember along with the promises.

When God directed Abram to leave, it was his season of change. When God spoke to Abram to move, it was not something simple, because even though we trust God, walking blind is no fun. Well, let's take a look at our brother Moses. I don't know how complacent Moses was, but it took fear to get him to move. Moses had committed a crime, and it caused him unknowingly to move into his place of leadership and become the deliverer God called him to be. What Moses did was not right, but God used it for his good. How many times has God had to allow something drastic to happen to get us to move?

We may have thought it was just the devil playing with us, but in fact, some of these trials God allows. We sometimes get so comfortable; we can't hear or see where God is attempting to move us. Maybe, just maybe, Moses was complacent with being where he was. Like us, Moses was out one day just checking things out, then the season changed. The season change caused Moses to run to his next season in life before being led to the backside of the mountain for a greater experience.

Like Moses, when we feel the wind blow our way, we need to grab ahold and move with it (Exodus 2:14, 15). Although it was an unfavorable incident that caused him to move, he moved. If we don't move, we will become like the rocks on the ground. When the wind blows, the trash on the ground will move, the leaves will change positions, and the trees will bow, but the rocks will never move.

Consequently, as the seasons change many times, the rock, if no one moves it, will remain. No matter how many times seasons change, the mountain may change shape, but it never moves from its place. Jesus is the rock, therefore, we don't need to be one. Jesus said, "Cast your cares upon me." Therefore, we can remain lightweight so that when the winds of God blow, we can shift with them.

CHAPTER FOUR:
The Set Place

Much opposition that has taken place in our lives has caused us to think twice about our salvation in Jesus. It has provoked many doubts, not only concerning us, but God also. In our minds, we wonder how God could allow these things to happen to us. Many instances, we wonder if it is all worth it. I can see the discouragement in this if we are not in the right season. Or we may be in the right season and have not yet learned how to operate in it. We are not going to move to another place until we have mastered the season we are in.

We don't enter into another season just to be there. God has something strategically planned for every season we enter into. There is a learning experience in every season. If someone gives a man a gun to use for protection and fails to teach them how to use it, it's no good when the enemy comes. If someone attacks them and they don't know how to use the gun, the first thing they will do is panic. The same is so when we are in an unfamiliar season. We can easily get discouraged when we have no idea where we are and what to do.

Once, I got so discouraged on this journey, I cried to God and said, "God, I don't know where I am, nor do I know what to do." I needed to listen to God to find my way so I could travel precisely on the path that was set for me. As each natural season arrives, we have to adjust our attire in order to feel comfortable. It is no different when the seasons change in our lives.

We may favor one season more than the other, but it does not negate the fact that we have to change with it. I am a winter person, and I operate better in the cold weather, but I still have to wear a coat, hat, and boots when the season arrives. If I don't, I will end up on a sickbed, feeling miserable, the way we feel when we miss God or are stuck clueless in a season. The change comes in our lives to make us who God wants us to be, not who we think we should be. Seasons don't come to give us notoriety and prestige. They come to humble us and give us wisdom, knowledge, and understanding. The seasons come to give us what we need, not always what we want. It's not about, "I want it, and I want it now." It's about walking out your season until you get to your destiny, promised land, set place, or place of favor.

Before entering into our next season, a chain reaction always takes place. We don't just freestyle into the next season. When the fall is setting in, the leaves change, and the air becomes a little brisk, alerting us of the season. When our season's change is upon us, many effects will take place. They may not all feel good, but it is necessary that they take place.

When we go from level to level in God, I would like to refer to it as trimesters of life before delivery. If we are going to be a deliverer of God's word in whatever fashion he sees fit, we have to adapt to the change. Although the hurts and pains we have felt and are still feeling seem degrading, we must realize that there is something God wants to do with that. I know what you are feeling is embarrassing and you want to throw in the towel, but you have to hold on, sister; help is on the way. I know what God has said about you, and it is not adding up, but you just wait and see what God has planned just for you. I know that everything you have tried has failed, but in time, it will resurface in a new light.

The hurt of your past is still fresh in your mind, but give it to Jesus; he can handle it. He can make you whole again. Jesus is the lover of your soul, sister. It may seem as though you will never get out of this situation, but it is only a test. Those mistakes you've made have taken you to a place of depression, but rebuke that demon and get in your position of power, girl! I know you are going through some difficulties, and you are wondering how God allows this.

The word of God tells us in Hebrews 4:15, "We have not a high priest who cannot be touched with the feeling of our infirmities." Therefore, we have not gone through anything that Jesus has never felt himself. The humiliation we feel sometimes seems more than we can bear, but just wait and see what God does with it. It is not all your fault that others see or saw you as some punching bag or a "touch me whenever you feel like" doll. No, it's not all right, but honey, it's all right because God is going to take that mess and turn it into a message. God is going to take every tear you have ever cried and reward you, not only materially, but spiritually also.

CHAPTER FIVE:

Where Does Your Strength Lie?

There have been many trials we all have gone through in life. There are trials we have shared with others, then there are some that others will never know about. We have had many accounts of disappointments, deceit, manipulation, you name it—some of us have been through a few or many. If we are honest, some of those experiences still sting a little when we think about them, but we have to push through them at all costs if we want to be victorious. Trials are much like a woman's labor pains; they travail until the child enters the world, then they forget the pain after they see the beauty of what has been produced. Although we want the pain to stop when we are going through difficulties, it never does until we have reached our place of destiny. Every rough place we enter, it is for a reason. God never takes us through trials just for the sake of it. It is to get us to the queen status we need to operate in. Many of us sadly will never operate in the queen status because we refuse to acknowledge that God knows what is best for us. Let God do whatever it is he needs to do to get the crown, sister. Don't be a Vashti; be an Esther. Let's do what we are supposed to do concerning the things of God.

In order to experience the original plan of God for our lives, he has to excavate everything that is not like him. Every piece of dirt and grime and unclean thing has to be removed. Just as an excavator carefully removes dirt from an archaeological site to discover the real mysteries, God has to remove all uncleanness from our lives. Gently, with the trials of life, he brushes them away little by little. God wants to make sure that in the process of uncovering the queen, nothing gets mishandled.

Over time, what we have allowed the world to suppress has to be carefully unveiled. The entire muddle of things we have allowed to snowball us has to be removed from our lives. We cannot totally walk in the greatness of God unless a change takes place. In order to hold the position of queen, we have to have queen status. This means that everything we think makes us queens needs to be excused right now in the name of Jesus.

What we think many times gives us power actually makes us weak. It is not the way we bat our eyes or the way we swing our hips that gives us power. It is not what we have on certain parts of our bodies that makes us powerful, although many of us think it's so. We are named the weaker vessel, but we have the power in God. (1 Peter 3:7) Because of what I had managed to get through I had a hard time agreeing with that. I thought I was strong because I tunneled through all these tough times and made it. Nevertheless, God showed me that no matter what I had been through, I was still the weaker vessel. The reason it seems like women are so strong is because in our frailty, we quickly turn to God for help. Therefore, when we grab hold of God, we grab hold to strength. We as weak vessels are operating out of the strength of God only. It may look like we are strong, but if we ever turn to another source of strength, it will show our frailty. Many of us will never wear the crown because we refuse to see what God has ordained from the beginning.

CHAPTER SIX:

Sold Out!

All we see is what reflects back at us from the mirror. What some of us see in the mirror is a recovering addict, a whoremonger, a liar, a cheater, an alcohol abuser, a former prostitute, a child abuser, a murderer, or a thief, and some of us may see a lonely, old woman. We never really see what God had intended, because we are too busy looking at the natural. What God wants us to see is far more than an image of this natural man.

We as people of God have allowed the enemy to talk us out of who we really are. We have allowed him to confine us to a life of nothingness, showing us only what our natural mind can conceive. He has voiced his opinion about who he thinks we are and how we should go about doing certain things. I concluded some time ago that I would no longer value opinions of others so much until I excused what God said about me. When we know who and whose we are, there is nothing anyone can say to change our minds.

When a queen sits on her throne, she sits poised and confident. She lets nothing and no one make decisions as to who she is. Her mind is made up, because she is the queen. She wears the crown filled with jewels and layered with gold, and the tips thereof sparkle. A queen takes charge of her life, directs others, and demands respect; she is served because she is royalty. All of these descriptions make us want to straighten our vertebrae, lift our chin, throw our hair back, and spread our nostrils. But wait! Before you do those things, listen to what a queen really is and does. The first thing a queen does is give herself away. We gave ourselves away to the natural man when we were in the world, so why not give ourselves away to God? Remember at the beginning of the chapter when I mentioned the fact that a queen first gives her life to Jesus? OK, then it is imperative that we totally trust him with every single part of us, withholding nothing. He needs to deal with the whole person in order to give complete results. A queen does not give one half and leave the other half to do as she pleases; this will cause spiritual schizophrenia. When a queen gives her all, withholding nothing, she is making a conscious decision to take control of her life. Taking control of your life consists of giving it to Jesus totally. We can never really direct others if we ourselves are not in our places of authority. We cannot demand respect from others if we don't respect ourselves. When we respect the life and relationship with Jesus, it will provoke others to respect us. In order to sit on a throne, God has to sit on the throne of our hearts. When God is sitting on the throne of our hearts, everything we do will prosper in its time. A real queen doesn't want to be served; she herself is called to serve. As she serves God, she is a service to others, sometimes unaware. All she is as God has fashioned her oozes out little by little. She is time-released, releasing God's greatness when needed. She gets so lost in serving God that serving others becomes natural to her. She does not gloat on the service of others. She becomes royalty unaware, and her service provokes others to aid her. When we lose ourselves, we gain so much more in life. The jewels she wears in her spiritual crown consist of humbleness, respect, love, kindness, holiness, patience, long-sufferings, etc. The gold that layers the crown is the anointing placed in her life from the trials and tribulations she takes on. The sparkling tips of the crown are the effective work she has carried out. This is the life of a queen. If we are going to walk hand-in-hand with destiny and declare the promises are "yea" and "amen," we must walk out our season.

Part Four

CHAPTER ONE:

Highly Favored

To execute the works of the ministry, we no doubt need the favor of God in our lives. I asked the Lord what his personal look of favor was. His response was that it is the head nod of God to walk in his supernatural grace. When God gives us the head nod, this means that he will be with us no matter what comes in the attempt to carry out what he has assigned to our lives. If God gives us the right of way to do something, his power is also given. He stands behind and walks in front of whatever he tells us to do. All we have to do is be faithful as he is faithful. In this walk, there are many exploits that will need the supernatural grace of God.

I know if God had not given me his supernatural grace to go into some places or given me supernatural grace to go through some things, I would be totally consumed. Although in many instances I wanted to give up, his grace was always sufficient for me. I'm not just talking about the lights that would sometimes be threatened to be disconnected or the groceries that got extremely shallow; I'm talking about "If you don't get me out, God, I won't get out, and I will lose my mind" kinds of places. Nevertheless, these situations were only to prepare me for the next thing.

I find that we want the favor of God in our lives, but we are not willing to have the backside-of-the-mountain experience. The backside of the mountain is the place we receive strategic instructions for a seemingly almost impossible task to accomplish. The backside-of-the-mountain experience consists of getting those instructions that make us want to back up and just be a door-keeper in the house of God. I know all too well how these experiences can be.

When God informs us that we are going to do great exploits, we must be equipped, and the backside of the mountain is where we must take our places. So why is it that we must be called to the backside of the mountain? The backside of the mountain is a place of transition and change. The backside of the mountain is simply God calling us aside to have a private session with us about the next task. When there is a great work assigned to us, God needs our undivided attention so we will get instructions for the task ahead and not be distracted. When Moses saw the burning bush, something that he had never imagined, it caused him to stop and pay attention.

There are times in our lives when God will cause a showstopper so we will pay attention to what he is about to say to us Many times, because we get so engulfed in our everyday events, we tend to miss God on many occasions. Therefore, God has to send something to get our attention. In the backside-of-the-mountain experience, there was no one around to tell Moses he was exaggerating or tell him he was losing his mind because of what he experienced.

There was no one to say, "Moses, if I were you, I would or would not do this or that." Neither was anyone attempting to tell him how he should handle the situation of the burning bush. There was no one telling him he should back up from the bush or he will get burned. The only ones there on the mountain were Moses, the bush, and God, and nothing else to distract him. When God realized he had Moses's attention, this was when Moses was given his first instruction: "Take off your shoes." This was an indication that Moses had to take a different approach to the rest of his journey. Moses could no longer treat his journey the way he normally did. If God is taking us to another level, this means that it is imperative that we change the way we walk in his presence.

We cannot approach life in the same manner as we did before. This is one of the reasons we are stuck and frustrated in the ministry, or even life for that matter. We often assume if it worked in this season, it will work in the next season. Let me ask you something, if I may. Will you or will you not need an overcoat in ninety-degree weather? First of all, you are going to look stupid, and the next thing is, you will probably faint at some point.

These same things will happen in our spiritual walk. We want to wear the same anointing in one season as we did in the last season, and we are fainting because it is not working for us. What we did when we were kids will not work for us now.

We have matured, and now we have to do mature things. I know many times we want to be safe where we are, but we must move. God knows what it takes to move us to another level, and believe me, he will use it to the fullest. I don't know what your burning bush was or is, but mine was God allowing friends and family members to cast me aside and scandalize my name. My burning bush forced me into hiding away from everybody, right where he wanted me. This is not to say that my family and friends are evil, but he will use spiritual dysfunction to move us. What I did not realize was that God had allowed their dysfunction to get me to the backside of my mountain to get my attention. No matter how much I love my family and friends, God will sometimes use them to push us where we need to be to get his matters attended to. God will use the closest people to our hearts to get the oil out of our lives. There was a mandate on my life, and the only way I was going to carry it out was God allowing these things to happen. God permitted these occurrences to happen so that I may go back and lead others he had assigned to my life out of bondage..

CHAPTER TWO:

Trust God and Go!

The bondage is sometimes of suicide, homosexuality, low self-esteem, drugs, haughtiness, confusion, adultery, anger, forgiveness, hopelessness, or bitterness. Nevertheless, I had to go to the backside of the mountain to get all I needed for the journey. I had to be isolated in order to get strategic instructions for this journey, because God will not allow us to go into the enemy's camp unprepared. Although it was a lonely journey, I had to take it anyway. I took it because this was what God wanted me to do.

I took it because I loved God, and because he chose this journey, I knew the outcome would be above and beyond anything I could ever imagine. Isolation is never popular for us, but it is necessary. Another reason God isolates us is so the enemy can't detour us or slow us down. Some of us, I'm afraid to say, can't stand the fact that we have to be isolated from others. It sometimes almost sends us into a panic if we can't talk to our friends on the phone or stay on Facebook for hours reading and responding to posts.

It may have never occurred to us that friends and family can sometimes be a hindrance if we are consumed with them. If we can't stand to be away from friends and family, then we will not accomplish all God has for us, because some assignments require isolation. In isolation is when God shows us another side of him. God is a seasonal God, and when we see him in one season, he is ready to show us another season of him.

When God sent Moses to Egypt, he was setting the stage for deliverance for the children of Israel and to show the pharaoh who he was for real. Although when Moses got there, he ran into a number of disappointing scenes and began to question God, God explained to Moses that to Abraham, Isaac, and Jacob, he showed himself to be a mighty God, and he had not displayed to them that he was Jehovah (Exodus 6:3).

In essence, God tells Moses that his forefathers never saw him as a self-subsisting God, meaning that he is a permanent God that cannot and will not be moved. God revealed to Abraham, Isaac, and Jacob one side of him, but they had never seen the side that he showed Moses. In order for God to show us different sides of him, we have to be willing to take the test that affirms our favor. When Moses was sent to free the children of Israel from the hand of the pharaoh, he did not just go in and lead them out.

There were a number of confrontational endeavors he went through before leading them out of Egypt. There were times when Moses became frustrated because things didn't happen the way or as fast as he thought they would. He was already afraid, and he was hoping he would be in and out and it would be over, like many of us think today. Moses did not realize that God was favoring him with great levels of trust and faith in him. He was showing the pharaoh who was greater and letting the children know that he heard their cry. So, what must happen in all of this is evident: that controversy must take place before deliverance. The wind blows and shakes dead leaves from the tree. The wind is an indicator that something is happening in the atmosphere that we can't see, but we must have faith that something is happening.

If we are in a place of transition or taking someone else through a place of transition, there will be a shaking of the tree. The tree has to be shaken, because there are entities in our lives that must be dealt with. Sometimes the shaking is not comfortable, but we have to endure it in order to accomplish what we were sent out to do. It takes time, and there is nothing we can do about it except go with the flow. The more we go through, the more favor we obtain from God. Therefore, we must be ready to take on that season, and sometimes it calls for isolation.

We never know what we can do until God shows us who he is and what he has called us to do. We do it in his grace and power anyway. We just have to have the zeal for him and his ministry to accomplish what he has assigned to us. I find the reasons some ministries fail is because they don't allow God to finish the work in them before they step out into this vicious world.

We do as Moses did: we fuss and complain to God about what we can't do or what others are doing. God had to deal with Moses about his fear and doubt before he could go to the pharaoh. God had to prove to him that he was God and that the children of Israel would come out of bondage. God also had to frustrate Moses with the junk, talking of the pharaoh and the grief of the children of Israel and the magicians before he would show his power. Oftentimes, God will allow frustration to come in order to get his mission accomplished. Many of us will never move in God until we are sick and tired of a thing. When the children of Israel showed Moses their frustration, it made Moses question God about the condition of the children. It was in Moses's frustration that God started the final process. I myself, and I am sure you, have experienced wanting to give up on the process before it started because it seemed too hard. In Moses's frustration is when the curtains opened up and the show started for him. It seemed many times that God had left Moses to look like a fool because the magicians were performing the same acts as Moses were, but God would peep his head in every now and then to encourage Moses.

Moses went from doubting to waving his rod to part the Red Sea. I can imagine Moses thought God had forsaken him because of all he was going through. But God showed him that he was with him all the way. Eventually, Moses was able to see God as no man had seen him before and was eventually permitted to write those Ten Commandments we should live by today.

Moses did a great work for the Lord, but it took the backside of the mountain. Walking in greatness consists of selling out for God so he can do what he wants to do in our lives.

After we have gone through the necessities of trials is when the blessings of God start to flow in our lives. Every great man and woman have to be prepared in one way or another.

CHAPTER THREE:

Boot Camp

I would often wonder why the prayers I asked to be answered were never manifested, and I would get frustrated. It is not that the prayers were not answered; I had to be pruned for them. I had to be given the supernatural grace to get through whatever was needed to receive what I had asked. When God has blessings beyond measure for us, we must be conditioned for them. Anyone can walk up to us and give us fifty dollars, but they could never out-give God when God has millions and billions to extend to us. We are conditioned to handle fifty dollars, but millions and billions, we have to be conditioned for, and this is where the supernatural grace comes in. There will be numerous occasions where God will take us to a place to pull out of us what we need for this journey. he Lord expresses his love for us and declares what he has planned for us because he possesses knowledge of what we need. Jeremiah 29:11 says that whatever we need, God gives; therefore, we must be prepared to take all he has for us. As we have seen in Moses's time, preparation is not always a favorable action, but it is much needed. Just because we agree with

God concerning the ministry does not mean we are off the hook concerning the trials.

There are times that we ask God in prayer to give us what we need for the ministry, but we don't realize some of these necessities are somewhat distasteful to the flesh. For instance, some of us have the need for patience, therefore, God will place us in a position that will try our patience to the limit, but we must stay in this place of grooming until it's flawless.

When God gives to us from his arsenal of greatness, he goes all the way. God does not lose the reins because we are crying about the pain of the process. God knows what we need, and when we agree to do the works of the Lord, he does not stop his training until we are good soldiers of his army.

When we think of the word *favor*, the first thing we think of is material gain, and we feel as though we have the right to square our shoulders back. There is nothing wrong with material gain, because in the end, this is our reward. There are small acts of favor that cost a little, then there are favors that cost everything. The favors that cost little are those things that take little to no effort to do. If I could use the example: "Do me a favor and hand me that book on the other side of you," all it takes is a lean and a stretch and it's all over. The act of favor that was given to me didn't need to be earned, because nothing would come out of it but a minimal movement. It was not life-changing, and nobody's life will change because of it.o On the other hand, when it comes to the gospel of Jesus Christ, it's another story. Moses led many out of bondage because he was given supernatural grace to go through difficult situations.

When Moses saw the state of mind and the severity of the bondage of the children of Israel, he was hurt, confused, and somewhat angry. He questioned God about his mission, but because God had showed him his power before, he stood on God's word. What Moses didn't know was that what he experienced in the beginning of the mission would be the last thing he would experience before the great parting of the Red Sea.

As God takes us to difficult places and puts us through difficult tasks, it always gets very frustrating before the parting of our Red Sea. We are all assigned to certain people; therefore, we must be ready and take necessary measures to get the job done. I encourage you to take the backside of the mountain, not only for you, but also for others that are waiting for you to lead them out of whatever the enemy has trapped them in. God gave Moses the head-nod to be a deliverer of his people, and Moses accomplished his mission. What about you?

CHAPTER FOUR:

It's Not About You

Let's look at Queen Esther, who was chosen to save the Jews—and her own life, for that matter. If Esther were never chosen, Haman would have had his way and would have summoned others to kill all the Jews because of his haughty and angry spirit. However, because Mordecai made a conscious decision to enroll his niece at the palace, and because Esther was willing to comply, favor was given, and lives were saved. Esther was quickly chosen to meet the king, and there are evident reasons why she was chosen so quickly. The favor of God was given to Esther because she was humble and she knew her place.

Oftentimes, we are looked over because we sometimes move too fast or we put ourselves in places we think we should already be. Esther waited for the timing of God before she approached King Ahasuerus. There is a timing we should apply ourselves to in order for God's perfect will to manifest.

After the purification process was over, she was asked what more she needed to come in to see the king. Esther did not make a list a mile long, because she was chosen. She was probably surprised and shocked she was even chosen. I guess she was just happy to be in a good place in the palace. In Esther 2, it seems that Esther felt that just being able to get her foot in the door was enough for now.

Nevertheless, Esther was on an assignment. When Queen Esther entered the palace, she had no idea what she was going to face. She may have thought that she was just lucky enough to be the queen, but God had given her favor to eventually save the Jews. There are places we are in that we may feel we don't deserve to be, but we are in these places for a reason. When God places us in different areas, it is solely for his purpose. Yes, we may benefit from it, but still, he gets the glory. The queen and her people were facing death, and at some point, she would have to take a chance of going to the king out of the timeframe allotted and to conceal her identity in fear of someone knowing who she really was.

Sometimes, when someone else's life is on the line besides our own, we have to go against the grain to accomplish the mission. It does not matter what anyone says; we just have to follow the instructions of God. After the bad news of the Jews possibly being eradicated, her uncle Mordecai was in distress outside in sackcloth and ashes, screaming and crying in the middle of the city.

When Mordecai found out there was a bounty on his head, he was in great distress. He sent word to tell Esther she was in a position to put a stop to all this madness. Although it was not Esther's time to see the king, Mordecai enlightened her that it was her time to be in the palace to save the Jews. He also brought her to the reality that just because she was in the king's castle did not mean she would escape death (Esther (4:13)

When the favor of God was given to Esther to enter into the palace, all hell broke loose. Nonetheless, when it was all said and done, Esther was the queen, and her uncle was given a royal act as his adversary was forced to escort him around the city in the king's attire. When God has given us favor to do something, there is nothing anyone can do to move us as long as we follow his instructions.

When God's favor is in your life, it does not make a difference how long you have been in a truncated position before someone sees the favor in your life and chooses you for greater. As God places his favor upon our lives, it is not for the pleasure of looking good or thinking we are extra special. We are placed in specific areas to do a specific task, and we need the favor of God to do it. In my experience of God in this area, he gives us grace (favor) to sustain us in difficult places so when our time of reward comes, we won't be haughty and prideful and think we have arrived.

There may be a detailed job we desire or a place we want to live, but we must realize that just because we don't get it right does not mean God does not want us to have it. We have to make pit stops before we obtain the promise of God that is "yea" and "amen."

CHAPTER FIVE:

A Precious Jewel (Favor)

We oftentimes talk about the favor of God on our lives as if it is something we wear around our necks like jewelry. We want to wear it as a badge of honor as if we are more special than the next person. Although favor is given, the glory that projects from it belongs to God. The favor of God may be the only Christ some will ever see. We are placed in different lines of battle so that we can obtain different ranks of favor.

In my experience on the battlefield for people, I found that if it was not for the favor of God on my life to help those people, I would have left them right where they stand. We all know how difficult some people can be, especially when we are assigned to them, because when we are assigned to someone, it is like having a newborn baby to take care of. We can't just walk away, because if we do, there will be consequences.

Many times, on assignments I wanted to make a deal with God to walk off and leave them, but God just gave me more favor to carry out the task to the end. God could have relieved me of my duties, but he loved me enough to keep me in a difficult place because he knew it would bring me great victories and favor. I never saw what I just spoke until just now as I wrote this, so thank you Lord! We have to be very careful as to how we ask God to get us out of something he has allowed us to be in. God has given me the wisdom to ask why I am in a certain trial, because I need to know, is it God or my negligence that got me there? When I find these things out, I will know to get further instructions on how to handle it. I need to know if I should change my attitude or if this trial is a must. Every unfavorable situation we get in is not the devil; God is responsible for some of them, only because he wants to show off in our lives.

As I read the story of Job over and over again, I could never understand why God would speak so highly of someone then allow the enemy to come in and take everything he had. For years, I could not understand why this had to be for Job. One day, I was in what I thought was a bad place, and I felt like Job. I had lost everything except my mind, and I thought I was going to lose that at any given second. The spirit of the Lord took me to Job one day as I sat in a motel room, wondering what was going on in my life and how I got there. Again, I wondered how God could allow this for Job. I got the nerve to read the book of Job I asked God about his actions toward Job.

I asked God why he allowed this to happen to Job. God's response was this: Job knew me as provider. Now, I wanted him to see me as a restorer. After that answer, I was all right, because now I understood God wanted to show me another side of him, and the only way I would see another side was to allow God to perfect a certain level of favor on my life. Some trials are harder than others, but this is just an indication that the favor is greater, and this is not a cliché, because all the trials I have been through, I'm done with clichés. I don't make them, and I definitely don't want to hear them. I promise you; a cliché will do nothing but get your feelings hurt.

CHAPTER SIX:

Is That Your Oil?

When we think of favor, the first thing that comes to mind is favor to get material items, and we get excited. What we must realize is that we are watched and judged to see if we are worthy of the favor that is presented. When God sent Samuel to anoint Saul, there was taken a vial of oil. When David was anointed, there was taken a horn of oil. God knew Saul was going to go halfway and mess up, and he also knew that David was going to go all the way and hold his position as a great king. What we are able to endure and withstand determines the amount of favor that is put on our lives. The misconception of why some have the ability to do one task and others don't is because we lack the understanding of the word *favor*. We get confused and frustrated because we know what the word of God said to us concerning the signs, wonders, and miracles we are supposed to perform or the houses and cars we are to receive. What we fail to understand is we have to be equipped for it, meaning we are to be conditioned. If God allows us to operate without trials, we will totally mess up the whole scene of what we are supposed to be doing. This is what the trials and tribulations produce; they produce favor to execute these ministries and gifts. We must first understand the concept of favor before we get excited about the rewards. If we are excited about the rewards of favor only, we will miss them every time after we are put on the battlefield.

CHAPTER SEVEN:
Finish Your Assignment

In my early years of salvation, people would tell me that I had the favor of God on my life; it sounded good, and I felt some way about it, but I never really knew the cost. What they didn't tell me was that favor came along with many trials and tribulations. I did not know that potential favor would lead me to places of question and sometimes doubt.

What I did not know was God had to make me ready for what was to come. Many times, I would be confused as to why I got thrown in places and was not allowed to move until God released me. I would move from one place to another under the unction of the Holy Ghost, but I would question whether or not I did the right thing after the power of the Holy Ghost had subsided If there has been any kind of assignment on your life, you know what I am talking about. What I did not realize was that God was moving me from one assignment to another in order to condition me for the reward. God had to throw me in the deep waters and declare that I swim.

When we are chosen, we are never ready for what is to come to our lives for the sake of others. We are never ready for this assignment. That's why God never tells us what is going on until we get halfway through it. I remember one assignment I was on, I attempted to leave, but God's authoritative finger pointed me right back in place.

Later, after the mission was accomplished, he released me, and I found out that I could have done anything I wanted, and no one would have been able to move me. Although that was true, he hid that fact from me so I wouldn't mess up the assignment. Now, in my experience with God, I know that when God places us in an area for assignment, no one can move us, although in my life I have had a do-over, which was far from heaven because it was pure hell, but I made it by the grace of God.

There have been times when I told God that if he did not deliver me out of a certain task, I was going to get out myself. What I did not know was God put me in these situations so he could give me another level of favor. Although we move into some places of question, it's just God releasing his favor on us. When the favor of God is being released in our lives, there is a posture we must take in order to receive it, and some of these places may not be favorable, but we have to be there.

When a woman conceives and gives birth, she finds herself in the same position twice—only the second position is not so comfortable. In fact, it is a very painful position, but she must endure until the process is over. In the end, she will experience fruit of her actual labor. She is very happy with the baby boy or girl, and she forgets what she just went through. In all of this, she had to resume the position to get the manifestation of what she knew was already with her.

The Lord revealed to me some time ago that the anointing is already in its fullness in the earth, but it's according to us how heavy it rests in our lives. The more we get ourselves out of the way and yield to the obedience of God and take necessary measures the more it makes a path for the anointing of God to rest in our lives. We see many people; it seems that they can carry on effortlessly, and we admire that. What we need to realize is that this person has been a yielded vessel unto the Lord. One thing I realized is that we want the favor and anointing of God on our lives, but we refuse to get our agendas out of the way. As I stated before, the anointing is in its fullest in the earthly realm, but we must allow God to place us in these unfavorable positions so he can get the best out of us. When he places us in these areas, he will also give us his grace to go through. We will also get what belongs to us. The anointing of God is like a cape being draped on us as we go from level to level in God's anointing. When we reach one level of anointing, there is another level waiting to be placed upon us. It depends upon whether we are willing to receive it or not. Imagine someone putting capes on us one by one until we can hardly stand. This is what happens when God rests his anointing on us level by level. The more levels are placed on us, the more we are able to do in the name of the Lord Jesus Christ. It reminds me of when Joseph was given a coat of many colors from his father. I can imagine the colors symbolizing anointing on his life. We are anointed for many things, but we have to endure before it's displayed. Joseph had to encounter hatred and jealousy from his brothers, being thrown in a pit, sold into slavery, and being harassed by a whorish woman and accused of rape. The anointing to reign in the palace was on him, but he had to walk it out first. It may not seem as if we are moving into another place of favor because of the emotional distress we experience, but just know we are not moving—God is. Therefore, we have to stand still. When God finishes moving in an area in our lives, this is when he will allow us to move.

You see, God goes before us to clear the way for us before we are allowed to move. It's like God goes and moves the explosives from the minefield before we get there. One of the reasons we miss God is we are moving too much, and I can imagine God just looking at us saying, "Whenever you decide to sit down, then I will move. Both of us can't walk through the door at the same time because I am the one that leads the way." Just as John the Baptist made the way for Jesus, God makes the way for us.

Acknowledgments

First I want to thank the Lord Jesus Christ for affording me the knowledge to write these words to his people. To my friend Paul who has been very instrumental in this journey with me from the beginning. I thank my mother and father who have taught me in many ways about life and people. To my siblings whom I love so much, William, Milton, Samuel, Linda, Katie, Gloria, and my late loving sister Brenda, who had more faith in me than I knew. To my friends and sisters in Christ of many years, Carolyn, Katrina, and Dianne. Last but never least to my daughter Jackie, I love you and thank you for loving me.

www.ingramcontent.com/pod-product-compliance
Lightning Source LLC
LaVergne TN
LVHW012028060526
838201LV00061B/4519